A MUPPET™ PICTURE READER

Rizzo's Bike Sale

Written by Alison Inches
Illustrated by Rick Brown

Published by Big Tent Entertainment, 216 West 18th Street, New York, New York, 10011.

Hi, my name is  .

I am a  .

A sales  .

I sell  .

Old  .

A good sales

needs 3 things.

A nice .

A big .

And 1 more thing—

good .

Why? You will see.

Look. Here comes a girl.

I will sell her a .

I fix my 👔.

I put on a big 😁.

"Hi," I say.

"My name is Rizzo.

Do I have a 🚲 for you!"

"Here is a ,"

I say.

"It is pink.

It has a ."

"I do not want pink,"

the girl says.

"I want green."

"Here is a green .

It has a green ⚑,"

I say.

"This 🚲 is old,"

the girl says.

"The ◉◉ are flat."

"How about this  ?

It is green

and it is like new.

A little old 👵 rode it

to her 📬.

That is all."

"This 🚲 is too little,"

the girl says.

"Here is another ," I say.

"It is green

and it is like new.

And it is made for 2.

It has 2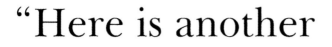

and 2 .

It is 2 times the fun!"

"I will give you

a free  too," I say.

The girl says,

"I do not need a

for ."

"So, what kind of

do you want?" I ask.

The girl points

to a .

It is green

and it is like new.

It has a shiny

and big 🚲🚲.

"I want that 🚲," she says.

"I want that <u>that</u> 🚲,"

she says.

"But . . .

that is my 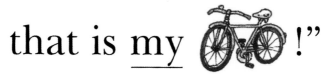 !"

I say.

The girl takes out

her  .

"OK?" she asks.

"OK," I say.

And that is why

a good sales

needs good .

So he can walk home!

rat	Rizzo
three	bike
smile	tie
shoes	one

flag	basket
lady	wheel
two	mailbox
horn	seat

bell	helmet
book	money
car	sun
bed	tree